Jr. Graphic African-American History

Black Civil War Soldiers
The 54th Massachusetts Regiment

Susan K. Baumann

PowerKiDS
press

New York

Published in 2014 by The Rosen Publishing Group, Inc.
29 East 21st Street, New York, NY 10010

First Edition

Editor: Joanne Randolph

Book Design: Planman Technologies

Illustrations: Planman Technologies

Library of Congress Cataloging-in-Publication Data

Baumann, Susan K.

Black Civil War Soldiers : The 54th Massachusetts Regiment / by Susan K. Baumann. — First edition.

    pages cm. — (Jr. graphic African-American history)

Includes index.

ISBN 978-1-4777-1316-7 (library binding) — ISBN 978-1-4777-1457-7 (pbk.) — ISBN 978-1-4777-1458-4 (6-pack)

1. United States. Army. Massachusetts Infantry Regiment, 54th (1863-1865)—Juvenile literature. 2. United States—History—Civil War, 1861-1865—Participation, African American—Juvenile literature. 3. African American soldiers—History—19th century—Juvenile literature. 4. Massachusetts—History—Civil War, 1861-1865—Regimental histories—Juvenile literature. 5. United States—History—Civil War, 1861-1865—Regimental histories—Juvenile literature. 6. United States. Army. Massachusetts Infantry Regiment, 54th (1863-1865)—Comic books, strips, etc. 7. United States—History—Civil War, 1861-1865—Participation, African American—Comic books, strips, etc. 8. African American soldiers—History—19th century—Comic books, strips, etc. 9. Massachusetts—History—Civil War, 1861-1865—Regimental histories—Comic books, strips, etc. 10. United States—History—Civil War, 1861-1865—Regimental histories—Comic books, strips, etc. 11. Graphic novels. I. Title. II. Title: 54th Massachusetts Regiment.

E513.554th .B38 2014

973.7'415—dc23

                                        2012049052

Manufactured in the United States of America

CPSIA Compliance Information: Batch #S13PK1: For Further Information contact Rosen Publishing, New York, New York at 1-800-237-9932

Contents

Introduction and Main Characters   3

Black Civil War Soldiers: The 54th Massachusetts
   Regiment   4

Timeline   22

Glossary   23

Index and Websites   24

Introduction

The Civil War began in 1861. The conflict between the North and the South centered on slavery. Southern states wanted to continue the practice and withdrew from the Union. When the war first began, African Americans were not allowed to join the Union army. This policy soon changed, and the 54th Massachusetts **Regiment** was one of the first Civil War units made up of African-American soldiers. The regiment fought in several battles, including at Fort Wagner, and gained fame for its bravery in battle.

Main Characters

Governor John A. Andrew (1818–1867) Governor of Massachusetts.

Sergeant William Harvey Carney (1840–1908) **Sergeant** in the 54th Massachusetts Regiment of the Union army.

Frederick Douglass (1818–1895) Famous black **abolitionist**.

Major General Quincy A. Gillmore (1825–1888) Commander of the Union army in the South.

Colonel Robert Gould Shaw (1837–1863) Commander of the 54th Massachusetts Regiment of the Union army.

Brigadier General George C. Strong (1832–1863) Military leader under Major General Gillmore.

BLACK CIVIL WAR SOLDIERS: THE 54TH MASSACHUSETTS REGIMENT

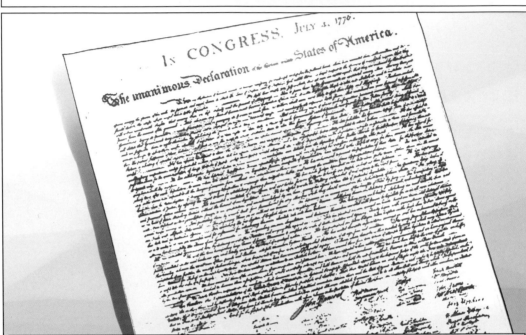

THE DECLARATION OF INDEPENDENCE, WHICH WAS SIGNED IN 1776, STATED THAT THE UNITED STATES WANTED ITS FREEDOM FROM BRITAIN. IT SAID, "WE HOLD THESE TRUTHS TO BE SELF-EVIDENT, THAT ALL MEN ARE CREATED EQUAL. . ." HOWEVER, PEOPLE DID NOT AGREE ABOUT WHETHER OR NOT THIS APPLIED TO THE ISSUE OF SLAVERY.

AS TIME WENT BY, THE NORTH AND THE SOUTH DEVELOPED VERY DIFFERENT ATTITUDES TOWARD SLAVERY. THE SOUTH DEPENDED UPON ENSLAVED AFRICAN AMERICANS TO DO THE HARD WORK OF GROWING CROPS, INCLUDING COTTON.

IN 1860, ABRAHAM LINCOLN WAS ELECTED PRESIDENT. HIS PARTY, THE REPUBLICANS, WAS AGAINST SLAVERY IN THE NEW AMERICAN **TERRITORIES**. PEOPLE IN THE SOUTH WERE AFRAID THAT SLAVERY WOULD BE **ABOLISHED** AND THEIR WAY OF LIFE RUINED.

STATES IN THE SOUTH BEGAN LEAVING THE UNITED STATES, OR THE UNION. THE NATION SPLIT INTO TWO SHARPLY DIVIDED GROUPS, AND THE SOUTH BECAME KNOWN AS THE CONFEDERACY. THE IMAGINARY LINE SEPARATING NORTH FROM SOUTH WAS KNOWN AS THE **MASON-DIXON LINE**.

ON APRIL 12, 1861, SOUTHERN SOLDIERS ATTACKED FORT SUMTER, IN SOUTH CAROLINA, WHICH WAS PROTECTED BY UNION SOLDIERS. THIS BATTLE STARTED THE CIVIL WAR. THE UNION LOST THIS FIRST BATTLE AND GAVE UP THE FORT.

PRESIDENT LINCOLN SIGNED THE **EMANCIPATION PROCLAMATION** ON JANUARY 1, 1863. THE CIVIL WAR WAS STILL RAGING, BUT THE ACT FREED THE SLAVES IN THE SOUTH.

THIS ACT IS THE GREATEST EVENT OF OUR TIME. IF ONLY EVERYONE AGREED WITH ME.

AT FIRST, THERE WERE ONLY A FEW BLACK SOLDIERS IN THE UNION ARMY. THEN, MASSACHUSETTS GOVERNOR JOHN ANDREW BEGAN FORMING A GROUP OF AFRICAN-AMERICAN SOLDIERS. IT WAS CALLED THE 54TH REGIMENT.

BLACK MEN ARE AS CAPABLE OF FIGHTING THIS WAR AS WHITE MEN. THEY ARE FIGHTING FOR THE FREEDOM OF THEIR PEOPLE.

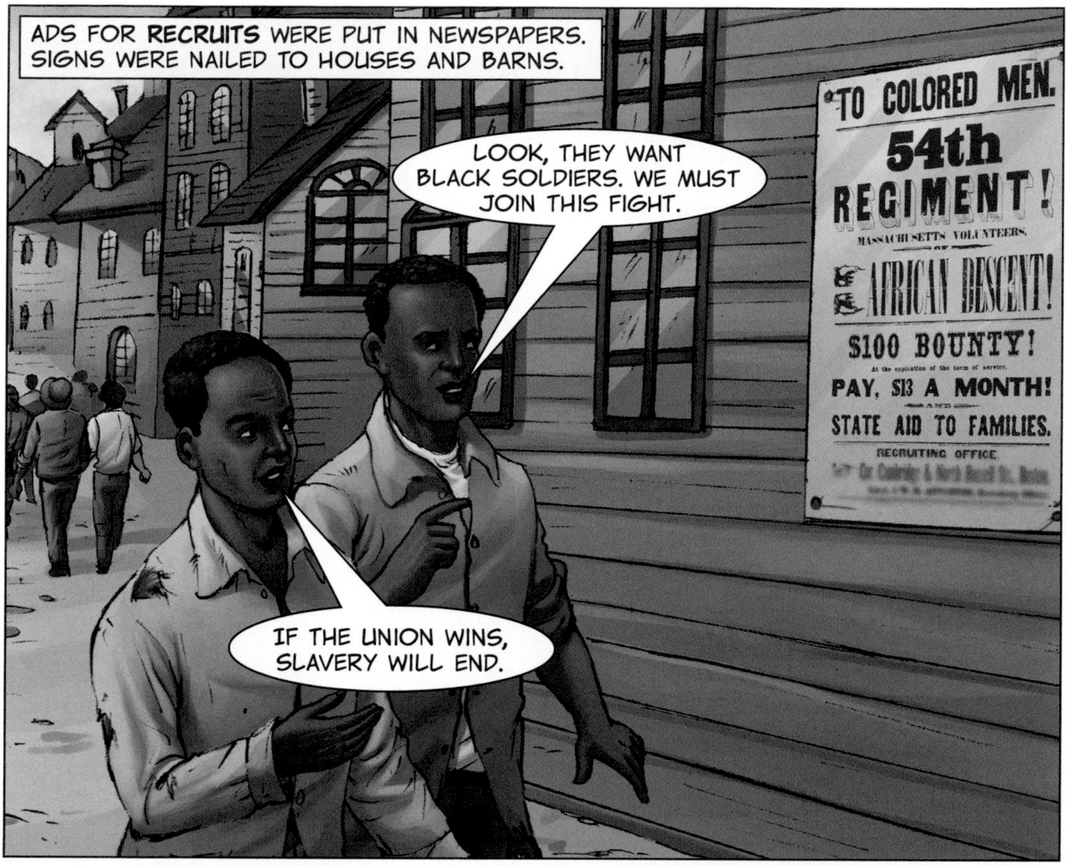
ADS FOR **RECRUITS** WERE PUT IN NEWSPAPERS. SIGNS WERE NAILED TO HOUSES AND BARNS.
TO COLORED MEN.
54th REGIMENT!
MASSACHUSETTS VOLUNTEERS,
OF
AFRICAN DESCENT!
$100 BOUNTY!
PAY, $13 A MONTH!
AND
STATE AID TO FAMILIES.
RECRUITING OFFICE
LOOK, THEY WANT BLACK SOLDIERS. WE MUST JOIN THIS FIGHT.
IF THE UNION WINS, SLAVERY WILL END.

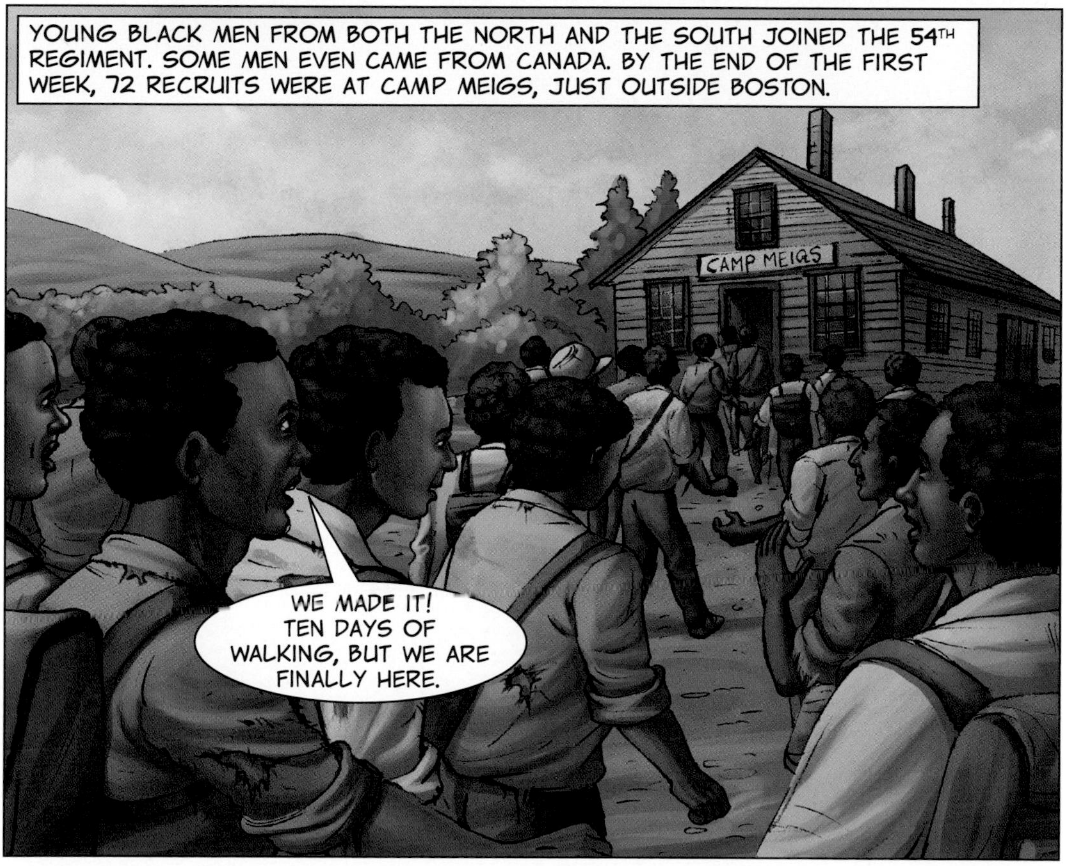
YOUNG BLACK MEN FROM BOTH THE NORTH AND THE SOUTH JOINED THE 54TH REGIMENT. SOME MEN EVEN CAME FROM CANADA. BY THE END OF THE FIRST WEEK, 72 RECRUITS WERE AT CAMP MEIGS, JUST OUTSIDE BOSTON.
CAMP MEIGS
WE MADE IT! TEN DAYS OF WALKING, BUT WE ARE FINALLY HERE.

MANY WELL-KNOWN BLACKS WORKED TO FILL THE RANKS OF THE 54TH. ONE OF THEM WAS FREDERICK DOUGLASS.

ONCE THE BLACK MAN HAS BEEN A UNION SOLDIER, NO ONE CAN DENY THAT HE HAS EARNED THE RIGHT TO BE A CITIZEN.

TWO OF THE RECRUITS WERE FREDERICK DOUGLASS'S SONS, CHARLES AND LEWIS.

I WANT TO BE PART OF THIS NEW EXPERIMENT.

SO DO I.

MANY WHITE NORTHERNERS DID NOT THINK AFRICAN AMERICANS COULD BE GOOD SOLDIERS.

DID YOU HEAR THAT GOVERNOR ANDREW IS STARTING A REGIMENT OF BLACK SOLDIERS?

SURELY THEY WILL NOT FIGHT IN THE WAR. MOST LIKELY, THEY WILL DO SIMPLE JOBS, LIKE DIGGING DITCHES.

EVEN THOUGH THE ENLISTED MEN WERE AFRICAN AMERICANS, GOVERNOR ANDREW CHOSE WHITE MEN AS OFFICERS.

I THINK BLACK MEN CAN BE GOOD SOLDIERS AND LEADERS. MANY WHITE PEOPLE DO NOT AGREE WITH MY VIEW. SO WHITE OFFICERS WILL LEAD THIS REGIMENT. WE WILL SEE WHAT THEY ALL CAN DO TOGETHER.

THE GOVERNOR LOOKED FOR OFFICERS AMONG THOSE WHITES WHO FOUGHT AGAINST SLAVERY.

THERE HAS NEVER BEEN A GROUP AS COMMITTED TO VICTORY AS THIS REGIMENT. THEY WILL FIGHT AS WELL AS WHITE SOLDIERS.

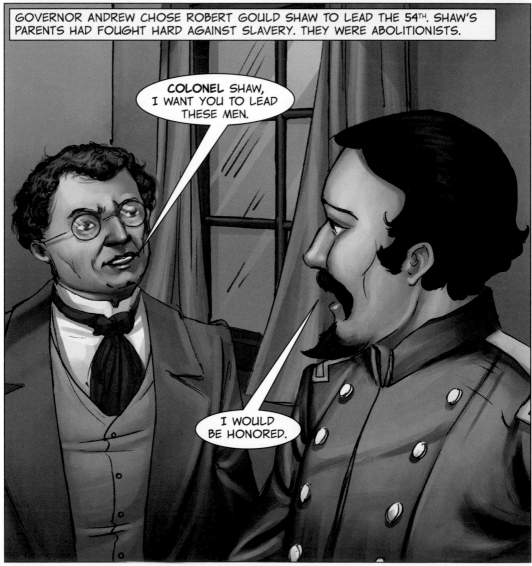

GOVERNOR ANDREW CHOSE ROBERT GOULD SHAW TO LEAD THE 54TH. SHAW'S PARENTS HAD FOUGHT HARD AGAINST SLAVERY. THEY WERE ABOLITIONISTS.

COLONEL SHAW, I WANT YOU TO LEAD THESE MEN.

I WOULD BE HONORED.

WHEN COLONEL SHAW FIRST SAW HIS TROOPS, THEY WERE A RAG-TAG LOT.

AT FIRST, IT WAS HARD FOR THE MEN TO MARCH IN TIME WITH ONE ANOTHER.

THE MEN **DRILLED** UNTIL THEY WERE ABLE TO MARCH TOGETHER PROPERLY.

THE MEN ARE LOOKING SHARP.

WHAT AN IMPROVEMENT!

AT LAST, WE WILL BE ABLE TO FIGHT IN THE WAR.

I NEVER REALLY THOUGHT THAT WE WOULD BE ARMED. CAN YOU BELIEVE IT?

THE MEN WERE GIVEN UNIFORMS. THEY ALSO RECEIVED THEIR WEAPONS.

NEXT, THE MEN LEARNED TO SHOOT THEIR **MUSKETS**.

KNOWING HOW TO USE YOUR MUSKET WILL HELP YOU SURVIVE IN THE HEAT OF BATTLE.

WE WILL SHOW THEM WE CAN FIGHT.

I CAN ALREADY HANDLE THIS MUSKET BETTER THAN OUR OFFICERS. I'VE BEEN HUNTING FOR A LONG TIME.

BY MAY 1863, THERE WERE 1,000 ENLISTED MEN IN THE 54TH REGIMENT. THERE WERE 37 WHITE OFFICERS.

GOVERNOR ANDREW PRESENTED THE 54TH WITH ITS FLAG. THEIR HARD WORK HAD PAID OFF.

CONGRATULATIONS, MEN. YOU ARE NOW SOLDIERS IN THE UNION ARMY.

THE 54TH PROUDLY MARCHED THROUGH THE STREETS OF BOSTON 10 DAYS LATER. HUNDREDS OF CHEERING CITIZENS CAME OUT TO SEE THEM.

I WONDER HOW THE BLACK SOLDIERS WILL DO IN BATTLE.

WE WILL SOON KNOW.

THE ARMY NEEDS ALL THE HELP IT CAN GET.

THESE ARE BRAVE MEN. THEY WILL SHOW IT IN BATTLE.

THE SOLDIERS TRAVELED BY SHIP FROM BOSTON TO THE COAST OF SOUTH CAROLINA. BY EARLY JUNE, THE MEN WERE IN THE MIDST OF THE WAR.

THE MEN OF THE 54TH TOOK PART IN A RAID ON THE TOWN OF DARIEN, GEORGIA. THIS WAS THE FIRST TIME THEY WERE INVOLVED IN COMBAT. IN THE END, THE TOWN WAS COMPLETELY DESTROYED.

IF WE CAN KEEP THE SOUTHERNERS FROM GETTING FOOD AND WEAPONS, WE CAN WIN THE WAR.

THE MEN FIGHT WELL, BUT I DO NOT SEE HOW WE CAN CLOSE THE HARBOR.

GENERAL QUINCY GILLMORE LED THE UNION FORCES IN THE SOUTH. HE WANTED TO TAKE CHARLESTON HARBOR, IN SOUTH CAROLINA. THE CONFEDERATES DEPENDED ON THE HARBOR TO GET SUPPLIES BY SHIP.

MORRIS ISLAND, RIGHT IN THE HARBOR, IS THE KEY.

IF WE TAKE THE ISLAND, WE CAN KEEP SOUTHERN SHIPS FROM ENTERING THE HARBOR.

THE 54TH WAS ORDERED TO ATTACK JAMES ISLAND. AT THE SAME TIME, OTHER UNION SOLDIERS WERE ATTACKING MORRIS ISLAND. THE JOB OF THE 54TH WAS TO DRAW ATTENTION AWAY FROM THE MORRIS ISLAND ATTACK. THE MORRIS ISLAND ATTACK FAILED, BUT THE 54TH SAVED MANY SOLDIERS' LIVES.

GENERAL GILLMORE PLANNED ANOTHER ATTACK. THE UNION WOULD ATTACK FORT WAGNER. FORT WAGNER WAS ON THE NORTHERN EDGE OF MORRIS ISLAND.

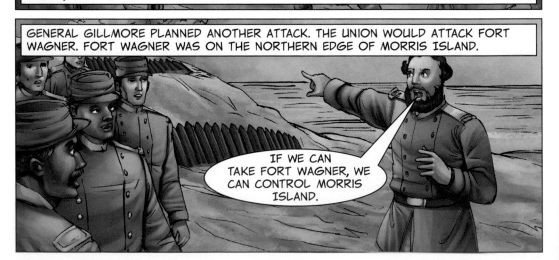

IF WE CAN TAKE FORT WAGNER, WE CAN CONTROL MORRIS ISLAND.

THE SOLDIERS WERE HUNGRY AND EXHAUSTED FROM THEIR BATTLE AT JAMES ISLAND. COLONEL SHAW KNEW THEY WOULD STILL FIGHT BRAVELY. HE WANTED THEM TO LEAD THE ATTACK ON FORT WAGNER.

SUDDENLY, BRIGADIER GENERAL GEORGE STRONG APPEARED OUT OF THE SMOKE. HE CAME TO SPEAK TO THE MEN.

BRIGADIER GENERAL STRONG ORDERED THE MAN CARRYING THE US FLAG TO COME FORWARD.

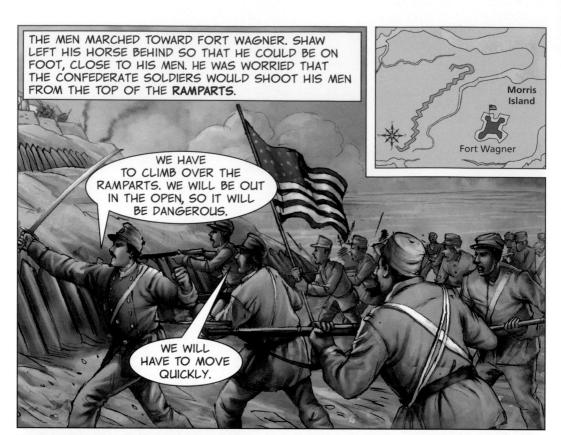

THE MEN MARCHED TOWARD FORT WAGNER. SHAW LEFT HIS HORSE BEHIND SO THAT HE COULD BE ON FOOT, CLOSE TO HIS MEN. HE WAS WORRIED THAT THE CONFEDERATE SOLDIERS WOULD SHOOT HIS MEN FROM THE TOP OF THE **RAMPARTS.**

Morris Island

Fort Wagner

WE HAVE TO CLIMB OVER THE RAMPARTS. WE WILL BE OUT IN THE OPEN, SO IT WILL BE DANGEROUS.

WE WILL HAVE TO MOVE QUICKLY.

THE SOLDIERS **SLOGGED** THEIR WAY THROUGH A WATERY DITCH, WHICH WAS DIFFICULT TO CROSS. THEY THEN SCRAMBLED UP THE RAMPARTS. MANY SOLDIERS WERE KILLED OR WOUNDED, BUT THE REMAINING SOLDIERS PUSHED FORWARD.

FORWARD, 54TH!

COLONEL SHAW LED HIS MEN IN BATTLE, WAVING HIS SWORD HIGH AND SHOUTING ENCOURAGING WORDS. AS HE WENT OVER THE TOP OF THE RAMPART, HE SUDDENLY FELL, FATALLY WOUNDED. SOME OF HIS MEN STOPPED TO HELP HIM, BUT IT WAS TOO LATE.

COLONEL SHAW HAS GONE DOWN!

WE CANNOT STOP NOW. WE MUST FIGHT ON IN HIS MEMORY.

WHEN THE FLAG BEARER WAS SHOT, SERGEANT WILLIAM CARNEY GRABBED THE FLAG FROM HIS HANDS.

I MUST CARRY THE FLAG NOW.

CARNEY RAN TO THE TOP OF A NEARBY SLOPE AND WAVED THE FLAG. ALTHOUGH MANY UNION SOLDIERS FOUGHT BRAVELY AT FORT WAGNER, THE UNION LOST THE BATTLE. FIFTY-FOUR MEN FROM THE 54TH REGIMENT DIED AS A RESULT OF THE BATTLE, AND MANY MORE WERE SERIOUSLY WOUNDED.

BOYS, THE OLD FLAG NEVER TOUCHED THE GROUND.

AT THIS SAME TIME, THERE WERE RIOTS IN SOME LARGE CITIES. IN NEW YORK CITY, BLACKS WERE BRUTALLY BEATEN AND EVEN KILLED. THESE WERE KNOWN AS THE CIVIL WAR DRAFT RIOTS. THE HEROISM OF THE 54TH HELPED SOOTHE RACE RELATIONS DURING THIS AWFUL TIME.

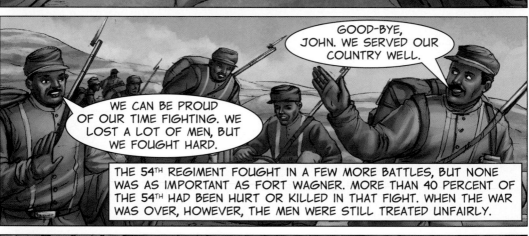

GOOD-BYE, JOHN. WE SERVED OUR COUNTRY WELL.

WE CAN BE PROUD OF OUR TIME FIGHTING. WE LOST A LOT OF MEN, BUT WE FOUGHT HARD.

THE 54TH REGIMENT FOUGHT IN A FEW MORE BATTLES, BUT NONE WAS AS IMPORTANT AS FORT WAGNER. MORE THAN 40 PERCENT OF THE 54TH HAD BEEN HURT OR KILLED IN THAT FIGHT. WHEN THE WAR WAS OVER, HOWEVER, THE MEN WERE STILL TREATED UNFAIRLY.

WE FOUGHT JUST AS HARD AS WHITE MEN FOR THE UNION.

SO MANY BLACK SOLDIERS DIED, JUST AS WHITE SOLDIERS DID.

WHEN BLACK SOLDIERS JOINED THE ARMY, THEY WERE TOLD THEY WOULD BE PAID THE SAME AS WHITES. SADLY, THE ARMY TRIED TO PAY THEM LESS. AT FIRST, BLACK SOLDIERS REFUSED THE UNEQUAL PAY.

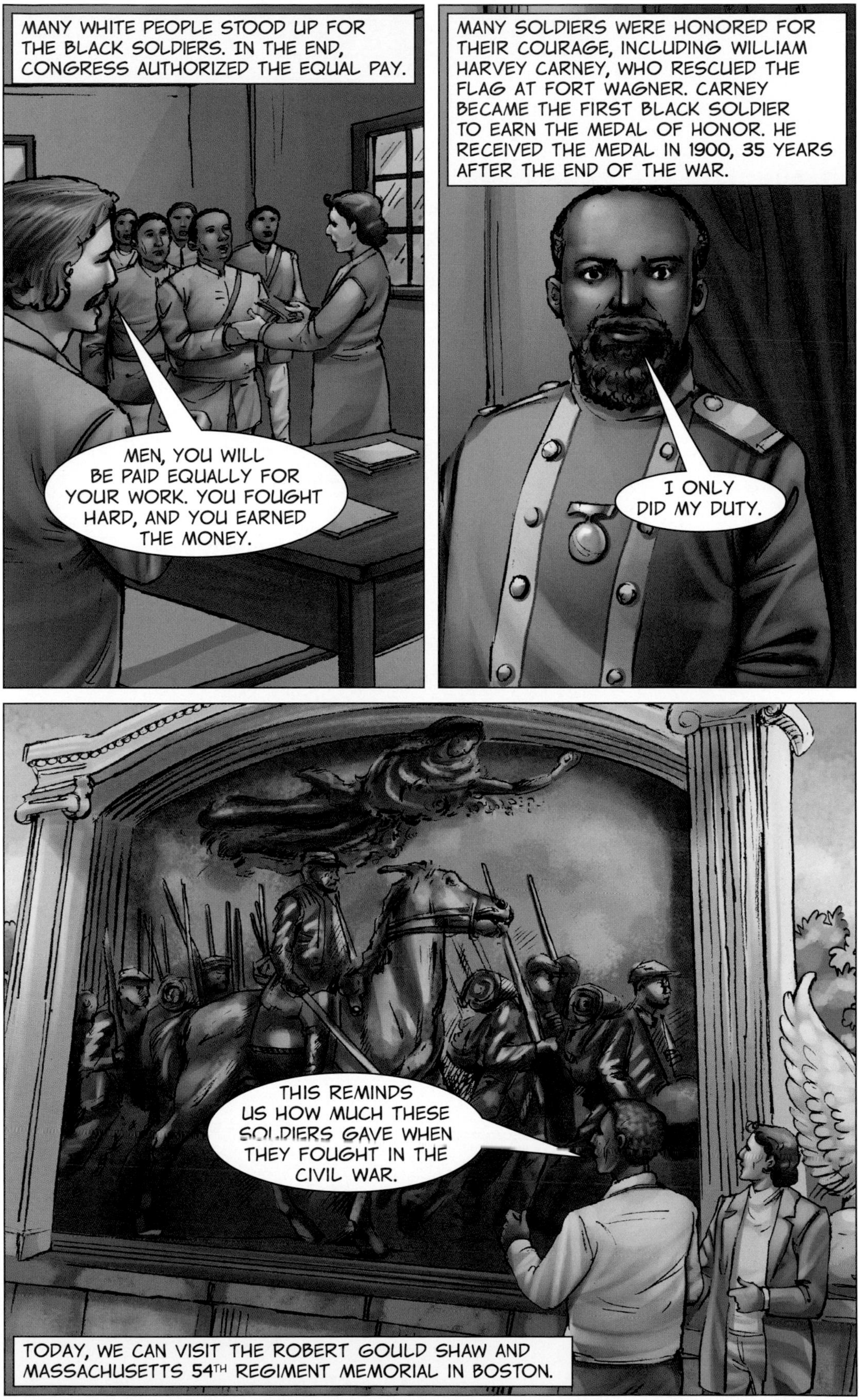
MANY WHITE PEOPLE STOOD UP FOR THE BLACK SOLDIERS. IN THE END, CONGRESS AUTHORIZED THE EQUAL PAY.
MEN, YOU WILL BE PAID EQUALLY FOR YOUR WORK. YOU FOUGHT HARD, AND YOU EARNED THE MONEY.
MANY SOLDIERS WERE HONORED FOR THEIR COURAGE, INCLUDING WILLIAM HARVEY CARNEY, WHO RESCUED THE FLAG AT FORT WAGNER. CARNEY BECAME THE FIRST BLACK SOLDIER TO EARN THE MEDAL OF HONOR. HE RECEIVED THE MEDAL IN 1900, 35 YEARS AFTER THE END OF THE WAR.
I ONLY DID MY DUTY.
THIS REMINDS US HOW MUCH THESE SOLDIERS GAVE WHEN THEY FOUGHT IN THE CIVIL WAR.
TODAY, WE CAN VISIT THE ROBERT GOULD SHAW AND MASSACHUSETTS 54TH REGIMENT MEMORIAL IN BOSTON.

Timeline

1837	Robert Gould Shaw is born to parents who are strong abolitionists.
1860	Abraham Lincoln is elected president of the United States.
April 1861	The Civil War begins.
January 1, 1863	President Lincoln issues the Emancipation Proclamation.
March 1863	The 54th Regiment begins forming and training.
May 1863	The 54th receives its flag from Governor Andrew and parades through Boston.
June 1863	The 54th arrives in South Carolina.
July 13, 1863	The Civil War Draft Riots begin. They last five days.
July 18, 1863	The 54th Massachusetts Regiment bravely attacks Fort Wagner but is defeated.
June 1864	Congress states that black soldiers should be paid the same as white soldiers.
April 1865	The Civil War ends.
1897	The Robert Gould Shaw and Massachusetts 54th Regiment Memorial in Boston is dedicated. The memorial shows Colonel Shaw with three rows of men marching behind him.
1900	William Harvey Carney receives the Medal of Honor.

Glossary

abolished (uh-BAH-lishd) Done away with.

abolitionist (a-buh-LIH-shun-ist) A person who worked to end slavery.

colonel (KER-nul) A military commissioned officer with a rank just below that of brigadier general.

drilled (DRILD) Did a set of repetitive exercises.

Emancipation Proclamation (ih-man-sih-PAY-shun pro-kluh-MAY-shun) A paper, signed by Abraham Lincoln during the Civil War, that freed all slaves held in Southern territory.

Mason-Dixon Line (MAYS-un-DIK-sun LYN) An imaginary line that divided the Northern states (the Union) and the Southern states (the Confederacy).

muskets (MUS-kits) Long-barreled firearms used by soldiers before the invention of the rifle.

ramparts (RAM-parts) Strong, protective walls, often with walkways, that usually surround a fort.

recruits (rih-KROOTS) New members of a group, often the military.

regiment (REH-juh-ment) A military unit.

sergeant (SAR-jint) An army or a marine officer.

slogged (SLOGD) Walked heavily through difficult terrain.

territories (TER-uh-tor-eez) Lands that are controlled by a person or a group of people.

Index

A

Andrew, John A., 3, 6, 9, 10, 14

B

Boston, Massachusetts, 7, 14, 15, 21

C

Camp Meigs, Massachusetts, 7
Carney, William Harvey, 3, 19, 21
Charleston Harbor, South Carolina, 15
Civil War, 3, 5, 6, 21
Civil War Draft Riots, 20
Confederacy, 5
Congress, 21

D

Darien, Georgia, 15
Declaration of Independence, 4
Douglass, Charles, 8
Douglass, Frederick, 3, 8
Douglass, Lewis, 8

E

Emancipation Proclamation, 6

F

Fort Sumter, South Carolina, 5
Fort Wagner, South Carolina, 3, 16, 17, 18, 19, 20, 21

G

Gillmore, Quincy A., 3, 15, 16

J

James Island, South Carolina, 16, 17

L

Lincoln, Abraham, 5, 6

M

Mason-Dixon Line, 5
Medal of Honor, 21
Morris Island, South Carolina, 16

S

Shaw, Robert Gould, 3, 10, 11, 17, 18, 19, 21
Strong, George C., 3, 17

U

Union army, 3, 5, 6, 8, 14, 15, 16, 19

Websites

Due to the changing nature of Internet links, PowerKids Press has developed an online list of websites related to the subject of this book. This site is updated regularly. Please use this link to access the list:

www.powerkidslinks.com/jgaah/war/